The Missing Harp & Other Children's Poems

Tara Williams

BookLeaf Publishing

Presentation by *BookLeaf Publishing*

Web: www.bookleafpub.com

E-mail: info@bookleafpub.com

ISBN: 9789357214049

First edition 2023

I would like to dedicate this book to my husband, Danny, and my two sons, James and Faiden. Believe in the power of your dreams.

ACKNOWLEDGEMENT

Thank you to BookLeaf Publishing. This is a dream opportunity.

And to my Mom and Dad, whom I miss every day.

Thank you to my favorite teachers, who opened up the world of reading and writing. The teaching profession is a labor of love, and you may not always see immediate results, but your time and dedication last a lifetime in our hearts and minds. Keep doing what you're doing.

The Missing Harp Part 1

An Angel cried from Heaven one day,
Interrupting a boy, busy at play.
"I wonder who's sad," the boy said out loud.
The angel came off of her fluffy, white cloud.
She cleared her throat, and spoke to the boy.
Her voice was so shaky, with no sign of joy.
"I am an angel. The Angel of Song.
But I cannot sing, for my magic harp's gone.
I am the voice of the wind in the willows.
I am the gush of the sound of the rivers.
I am the tune of the twinkling of stars.
I am the babble of the brook by the barn.
Out in the wilderness, I am the cry.
I play the 'Night's Silence' and the 'Moon's
Lullaby.'
I take requests. I've played a few.
Like 'Frost in the Morning' or 'Soft Drops of
Dew.'
I put my harp down and went off to play.
When I came back, someone took it away.
The 'Dance of Dusk' will soon have to be heard.
As will 'Slumber of Nature' and 'Nesting Birds.'
Without my harp, what will I do?
The world will go quiet. I'll get in trouble, too."

The Missing Harp Part 2

The Angel she cried, her tears turned to sobs.
She feared the worse, that her harp had been robbed.
The young lad did not like to see an Angel so sad.
He offered her all the help that he had.
"My friends and myself, will search low and high,
For the magical harp that you cannot find."

Under bushes with birds, around ponds with ducks,
They searched for a harp, without any luck.
It was late afternoon, and light became less.
The angel did know, it was time to confess.
She thanked the young lad, and left without song,
To tell Mother Nature about the harp being gone.
"Sweet Angel," Mother said when the truth was told.
"I took your harp when you ran off alone.
Your job was not done, but you went off to play.
Your harp was just tossed, not put away.
To teach you a lesson, I brought it with me.
I thought you'd miss playing your sweet melody.

I am not mad or angry with you.
Just please take care in the jobs that you do."
"Go my angel," Mother Nature said.
"Play your music. Put our world to bed."
The angel, she smiled, and hugged her mother.
She took her harp to play for others.
The songs of nature again were heard.
The twinkling stars and nesting birds.
When her task was done and mankind was
sleeping,
Angel took her harp to bed--
Just for safekeeping.
The End.

A Year of Haikus January

January one
Resolutions have begun.
Fresh starts are welcome.

A Year of Haikus--February

Love is in the air.
Fourteenth of February.
Cards. Flowers. Be Mine.

A Year of Haikus- March

March brings Saint Patrick.
Shamrocks. Rainbows. Pot o' gold.
Catch a leprechaun.

Year of Haikus-April

April is Easter.
Springtime, rain and thunderstorms.
Bringing forth flowers.

Year of Haikus-May

May is for Mothers.
Remember to celebrate.
Give gifts from the heart.

Year of Haikus-Summer

June, July, August
Summertime. Full of hot days.
Cool down at the beach.

Year of Haikus-September

September. School, again.
New pencils, freshly sharpened.
The bus comes early.

Year of Haikus-October

Halloween is near.
Haunted houses. Ghosts. Black cats.
Pumpkins. October.

Year of Haiku-November

Thanksgiving is here.
November brings cold, dark nights.
Holiday season.

Year of Haiku-December

December. Santa.
Boys and girls. Best behavior.
Gift giving galore.

The Messy Bedroom Part 1

I love my room,
The best part of home.
Mom says it's messy,
but at least I'm alone.
Outside my door,
My lil sis plays.
She's only four,
Always in the way.
She wants my time,
She wants my toys.
I want to read,
And think about boys.
I mean, I'm twelve years old,
That's practically grown.
I want private time, to be on my own.
My sister is little.
She pees in her pants!!
She smells like bananas,
Thinks she can dance.
My emoji for her would be
Eyes rolling upward.
If she were an elf on the shelf,
I'd hide her in the cupboard!
My room is my space,
Away from all that.

I don't let anyone in,
Except Chester, my cat.

The Messy Bedroom Part 2

My mom says it's messy.
What does she know?
I LIKE my clothes in a pile,
next to the stack of plates and bowls.
OK, MAYBE they're dirty
But it's not like it's gross.
They are licked clean,
Cause I mostly eat toast.
Sometimes there's cereal.
Oh, and ice cream, too.
They are orderly in their spot,
Between my clothes and shoes.
The Shoes! They are okay
just where they are,
Maybe not all together,
but their match is not far.
My books are stacked.
Kind of neat. In a pile.
By the bed. By the window.
By the sock-tower-compile.
My dresser isn't cluttered,
As some may think.
I NEED my makeup and hair brush,
the water bottles in shades of pink.
The bed! My bed!

It's the best part of my room!
I spend hours daydreaming
of my distant-future bridegroom!
Will it be Bobby from science?
Or Joey from math?
Maybe Dillon from English.
Or Danny from art class?

Enough about my sis and all my boys.
Here is the corner with board games and toys.

This is my room, all purple and blue!
Stars on my walls, that I stuck with gorilla glue!

Sparkly pillows and stuffies spread over the bed.
My collection of hats, to cover my head.

The tour is over, I hope you had fun!
Dinner's almost ready! Gotta get my homework
done!
The End

Imagine Heaven

If Earth is pretty with skies of blue,
Green, thick forests, and rainbows, too.

Imagine Heaven, and what it is like-
without pollution, poison, and people who fight.

Imagine the peace, the serenity and calm.
Imagine the love, understanding and charm.

Imagine the colors and smells and again, all the
love.
Imagine the ones we lost LIVING there and
watching from above.

My aunts Betty and Wilma both grandpa and
grandma;
My cats and my dogs and my white bunny called
Momma.

So love life and live large in all that you do.
Be kind and give yourself, all that you can.

Imagine Heaven. If Earth is good, Heaven is
GRAND!

Marshmallow

If I were a marshmallow,
I'd be squishy and soft.
I'd be peppermint pink,
Sugar-coated like frost.
I'd swim in your cocoa,
And float in your milk.
I'd toast over your campfire,
Then melt smooth as silk.
If I were a marshmallow,
How sweet I would be!
If I were a marshmallow....
Satisfaction guaranteed.

Best Friends

Many, many years ago we met,
And we are still the best of friends.
Time and life moved us apart,
Yet our bond will never end.
We've been together through it all,
From boys to schools to moves,
We had our ups, we had our downs,
But the universe approves!
We will be besties til the end,
I feel it in my bones!
In New York or Tennessee,
Or any other time zone!

Adventures of Peanut the Puppy Part 1

Peanut's a puppy.
He's tan. He's fluffy.
He is a chi-weenie.
His legs are so teeny.
Nothing stops him, though.
He plays in rain, sun or snow.
He has a best friend.
Their adventures don't end.
We call her Miss Jinx,
She wears a collar that's pink.
Her fur is soft black,
but her nails sharp as tacks.
She climbs trees in a flash
And runs quick like a dash.

Adventures of Peanut the Puppy Part 2

Together they find trouble and fun,
They dance, jump and run.
One adventure they thought was so great,
They missed their curfew and stayed out past eight.
Eight is Peanut's bedtime
That night, it was way past nine.
J and P went downtown.
Not sure what to do, they just looked around.
They found a theater that showed movies til late.
They watched one after another, didn't know it passed eight.
The animated show was their absolute fave.
Time was the last care they gave.
Not only was there a movie, they had snacks on the floor.
Drinks in the cup holders, Treats galore!
It was warm and so dark.
Peanut laughed so hard he barked.
They almost got caught but hid under the seat.
The movie theater experience was quite a treat.
They snuck back home and into their houses,
Their humans were sleeping with their snoring spouses.

No one knew about their movie theater outing,
They are currently adventure scouting.
The End.

Raccoons

They live in my yard.
Dark circles around their eyes.
Fingers to eat trash.

Miss Possum

25

Her tail is rat-like.
White fur. Fine and soft. Pink skin.
Eats ticks. Gentle animals.